Dreaming Sam Peckinpah

For John—

Who always enters
all houses justified.
Enjoy — Kip

[signature]

Dreaming
Sam Peckinpah

W. K. Stratton

ISBN: 978-0-9835968-7-5
Library of Congress Control Number: 2011936725

Manufactured in the United States

Ink Brush Press
Temple and Dallas, Texas

For

Tom Dodge, Frank "frankly" Parman,
and Kenny Walter (once again)

Also

Michael Adams, Dallas Baxter, Mark Belanger, Gar Bethel, Larry Bierman, Dan Bryan, Joe Bruchac, Bill Davis, Steve Davis, James Dickey, Don Duffy, Harry Ebeling, Bob "Uncle Punk" Ferris, Frank Finney, H.L. Ford, Pat Gallagher, Bill Gammill, Don Graham, Larry Griffin, Joy Harjo, Marilyn Harris (Springer), Arn Henderson, Lance Henson, Donald Hall, Jim Hoggard, Callie Jones, Jennifer Kidney, George Kimball, Skip Largent, Charles Levendosky, N. Scott Momaday, Brad Morelli, Emmett Phillips, Charles Plymell, Roxie Powell, Richard Reed, Carter Revard, William Pitt Root, Jim Sanderson, Betty Shipley, William Stafford, Glenn Todd, A.D. Winans, and Tom Zigal.

Other Books of Poetry from Ink Brush Press

Alan Birkelbach and Karla Morton, *No End of Vision: Texas as Seen by Two Laureates*
Jerry Bradley, *The Importance of Elsewhere*
Millard Dunn, *Places We Could Never Find Alone*
Chris Ellery, *The Big Mosque of Mercy*
Charles Inge, *Brazos View*
Steven Schroeder, *a dim sum of the day before*
Steve Schroeder and Sou Vai Keng, *a guest giving way like ice melting*
Jan Seale, *Nape*
Jan Seale, *New and Selected Poems*
Jesse Waters, *Human Resources*

For information about these and other Ink Brush Press books, go to www.inkbrushpress.com

CONTENTS

Note

Of course *The Wild Bunch* is the masterpiece, probably the greatest movie ever made. But *Junior Bonner* is the one that means the most to me. You have it all. Family strife. Family bonds. Questions about what it means to be a man. What it means to be a winner. What it means to be a loser. There is romance. Newly bloomed romance. Well seasoned romance. Flashes of anger, flashes of resentment. The wizened voice of experience. One nicely landed punch on a porch. A riproaring bar fight at the old Palace Hotel in Prescott. Hitting the road. And one fine bull ride. And something about the death of the West. And something about the death of the America I grew up in, the America I know the best, the America that's long, long gone.

But then there's Sam Peckinpah himself. He haunts me. He was of the generation of my father and stepfather, the World War II generation. He epitomized many of the ideals of the generation, even took them to extremes. At the same time, he rejected them. He was a sort of World War II generation grotesque. He was a Marine and seemed to possess the typical Marine's disdain for wimps. He saw horrible things in China just after the war wrapped. He knew violence first-hand. He smoked heavily. He abused his health in the way real men were supposed to. He had an impossible work ethic start work at four-thirty in the morning, go nonstop until after dark, then belly up to the bar and down whiskey like a *real* man. Single focus on the job at hand. To do anything less was to be, well, a wimp. Like a *real* man of his generation, he was not wrapped up in family matters it was the work that mattered. His relationships with women were a mess. But then real men of that generation weren't supposed to in tidy marriages. (But they damned sure were supposed to be the boss of the marriage.) He knew all about pieces of ass on the side. He knew the insides of whorehouses, especially ones in Mexico. He loved Mexico. He was an artist, a kind of poet who worked with metaphors created by visual images and lines of dialogue. He was an uncompromising artist, yet the pressures of his generational upbringing seemed to prevent him from publicly revealing a sensitive side. He never sold out, never took a cushy university position or a stable job in private industry. I doubt that he ever wrestled with insecurity. His art was everything, as I suppose it should be. He was a Westerner, cowboyed just enough as a kid to say he knew something about it. He never had much use for hippies, seemed largely ignorant of rock-and-roll, but he smoked dope and, eventually, snorted lines of coke. He grew a beard and hid behind shades. In the words of Faron Young, he lived fast, died young, and left a beautiful memory (at least, beautiful in ways).

As I've made my way through a half century (and more) of living, I've struggled with the examples set by Peckinpah and others of his generation. Most of the time, I've felt as if I've come up short by their standards even though many of their standards were horseshit. I've also been fascinated by the themes of Peckinpah's best work, the films bookended by *Ride the High Country* and *Bring Me the Head of Alfredo Garcia.* Big themes, important themes. The poems that follow (written over a thirty-year period) were not written in direct response to any of this. They've all come from my subconscious lyrical flow. Or whatever you want to call it. But, considered objectively, they bounce into and off of and around these things, these dreams of Sam Peckinpah.

W.K.S.

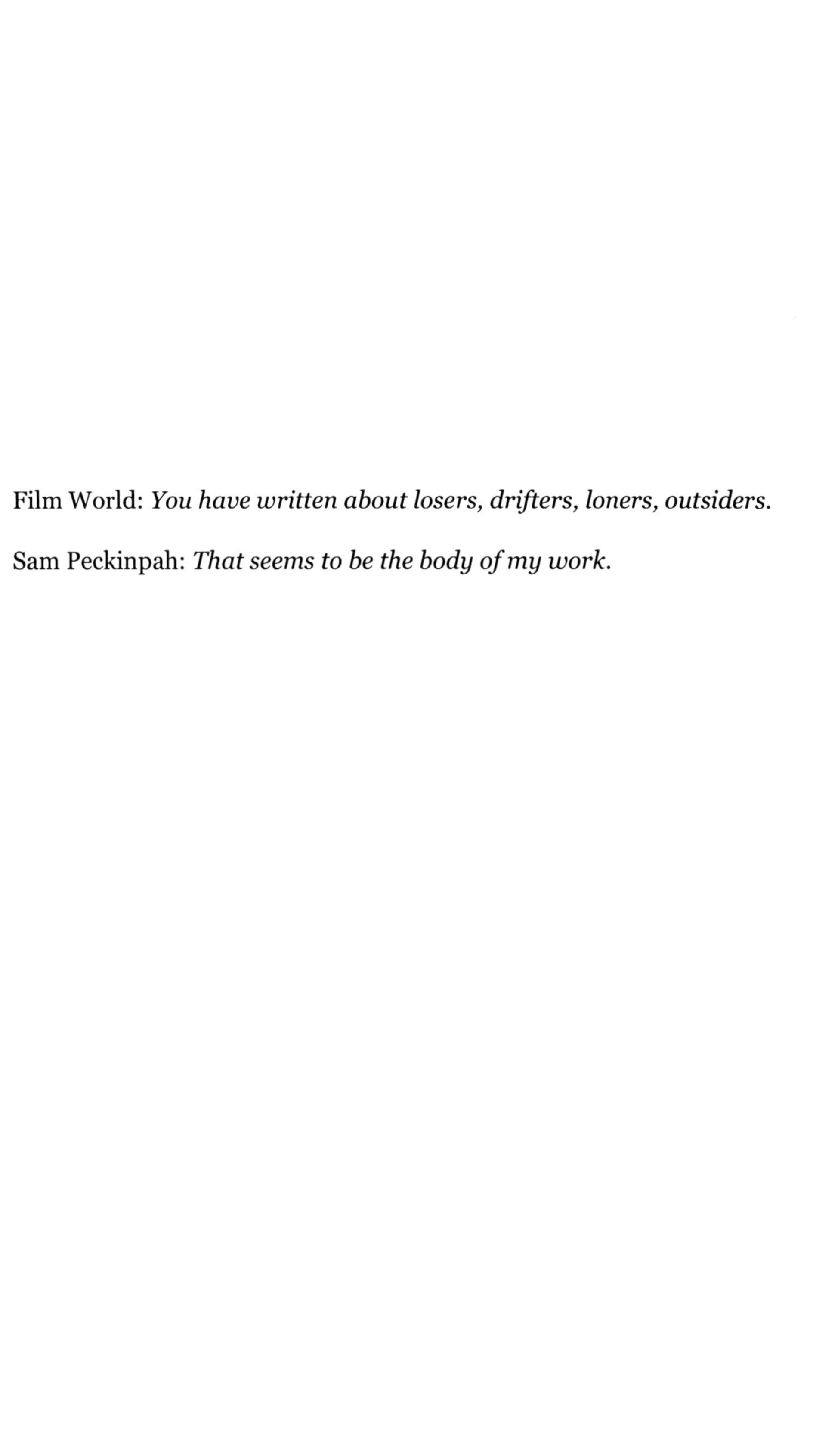

Film World: *You have written about losers, drifters, loners, outsiders.*

Sam Peckinpah: *That seems to be the body of my work.*

Boots: an Introduction

I had a pair of boots once. Rough-out leather, pointed toes.
Justin's. Fort Worth, Texas. I wore them everywhere.
Into Mexico. Into the Caribbean, U.S. Virgin Islands.
Into the Atlantic, Miami Beach. Into the Pacific, San Diego.
Into the Rio Grande, below Taos. I wore them in Los Angeles,
San Francisco, New Orleans, Laredo. I wore them into the
old Lone Star Cafe in Greenwich Village, boo-weed lid stuffed
down one of the uppers. I surrendered them to the custody of the
Deaf Smith County Sheriff's Department one night:
Thirty-six hours, drunk and disorderly.

They were good boots.

Now I sit in the suburbs, air-conditioned bubble. No one in my house
will speak to me. I drink beer from Peru, watch rented movies
Ballad of Cable Hogue first, then *Junior Bonner*.
Half asleep, dreaming Sam Peckinpah, dreading tomorrow,
back in an office, wondering how I lost the best part of myself.

I had a pair of boots once.

Good ones.

Part I

I am a child of the old west. I knew first hand the life of cowboys. I participated in some of their adventures and I actually witnessed the disintegration of a world.

—Sam Peckinpah

Answer

In morning
a yellow and black
bird flashes from
buffalo grass. Rocks
sweat mist five hundred
feet above the plain. Vultures
kettle between walls of
granite crevices. A rattlesnake
is a hose bulged with
hair and bone and
meat and blood.

And coyotes wait
for fire
for rain
for wind
for ice . . .

We must inhale these things.

Plan

One of these days I'm going to sell the
old house and head out to cactus country. I'll
stitch my oats into sand shoes and cut my hair;
I'll braid the hair into a belt and pull it
tighter as my belly hardens. I'll carry a
canteen and have one of those pocket kits to
test mountain pools.

One night and I'll lower my face into a lavender
stream and get a taste of trout logic.

One of these days I'll search for cowboys and
seek out the memory hidden in coyote songs.

Proper

In America you now speak in a tent about
versification. Your voice rains shadows of
dreams and minds of dreamers. Your voice
mists dead grass. Under a stone canvas
you have trouble deciding. You admit meandering.
What do you know of walnuts?
What do you know?

In the wind I smell white foam water
beneath the rocks. Black stains cling to
rock sides and linger. A leaf appears in this
treeless country. Your rain blocks my singing
these things.

What do you know of blood?

Texas Postcard

On their way to a job
at the evangelical church:
two white guys, Aggie caps,
golf shirts, riding in the pickup
          cab—

cell phones singing—

three *mojados* shivering in the bed
between the lawn mowers.

Letter from Tierra Amarilla

You could confine here: carve a *casita*
Straight into slanted stone and tongue the spring
Trickle down your living room wall. Rise up
At dawn to fetch gilded rays above pine

Detritus two thousand feet below you.
Everything wears away now. You are home.
You could re-find yourself here: place a crown
Of purple granite against the morning,

The wind your only music. Thunder curls
Beside you—it is your constant lover.
You beckoned deep into the brazos box
To draw it here above the troubled clouds.

Open your time to faint cactus and bleed
Across the sky. Everything rises to you.

Little America

Toothless woman—Need help cardboard sign—reclines
On the satin of asphalt, motorhome passing, no beer.

My mirror is soap scummed. Someone borrowed it.
I cannot shave, back my car, paint a soul.

She does not eat shrimp: hives. She does not work.
She smells everything. The moon breaks her nose.

Smoking room, only thing available. Yellow page love,
Only kind available. Cold water, diesel air: available.

Rental car anxiety outside Cheyenne. Little America gets
Me through. Sixteen days now, headache gone, waiting.

Oklahoma: 1928 (An Intentional Fragment)

i.

They come to this place tattered. They bury
Ears in red clay, breathe grass and gravel.

One is a white man or so he claims. He is
The color of old pennies, eyes wet walnuts.

He denies the soil within him. Fifty years and
He refuses the real story. He craves wind.

A piece of it: age five and he hits the tobacco fields,
South Missouri, which he pronounces *Massoura*.

Beaten by a stepfather named Jones, chewing
green tobacco to kill pangs: his education.

Age ten and he flees the cabin, walks to Kansas City,
Snow like his stepfather's whiskey breath.

Years pass in the hobo camp, rail rust on his face.
Hope flutters in the broken land to the west.

So: tattered he arrives and buries his ears.
This is a story about America.

ii.

Let us dig for the people in the earth. Let us breathe
Their wind, the wind he refuses. Let us sing with them.

We are children of the middle waters.
In the soil we stand above all others.

We grow corn and squash, lift berries and nuts,
We ride to the buffalo hunt next to the feather people.

We sleep warm in our trees. The others scurry
Beneath our souls. We love the French, loathe the Illiniwek.

Why does he deny us? This is a story about America.
And about a place of no towns and whining saws.

And about bushwhackers and hate preachers who slam their
Book and bang the beds. His denial spouts in that depth.

Begotten not made, his enmity surprises:
Only a nigger is worse than an Osage.

I ain't one, never was one, don't speak of it.
So soil people move, rebuked, silent.

iii.

Soil people surround him and know their brother.
He walks a ridge in bib overalls and newsboy cap.

You can find wind here, away from Missouri trees:
You can find wind and whiskey snow seldom breaks.

But he will not reveal his dirt. He is a rambler
And understands antifreeze intoxication. O that day!

That day of no light! Memories of a woman of odor
And colorless eyes. He awakens in her funk.

And there is no dawn, just bad liquor blindness. We sing
Of doctors here and their sad judgment, clawing for light.

Will I ever see the tattoo crooked against my left elbow?
Will I ever see a fiddle, a tank truck of gasoline?

Days pass and the light slowly returns. He never drinks
Again. He ponders Jesus and the blank unknowable sky.

This is an American story. Oklahoma: 1928.
Jesus is our friend. God is our nightmare.

iv.

Thanks be to God the Father for no rain and tumbling
Cotton prices and grasshopper invasions and tears.

He walks the Ponca City square, refuses to look
At his brothers drunk on antifreeze. Only niggers are worse. . .

He'll tell you this, tell you this his whole life.
He prods and works and studies, burning his being:

Hand-rolled cigarettes, Prince Albert in the can.
Ears full of clay and he considers driving wheels.

Maybe the railroad would have been best for him.
He met Jimmie Rodgers once in Temple, Texas.

That man was dead while he was alive, he recollects.
Nothing but bones and overalls and brakeman's hat.

Yet he himself is hardly more. He hacks and grabs Prince
Albert.
I never once heard him sing, whistle, or even hum.

Flames leap from the Ponca City refinery. This is America
So he puts on his cap and shuffles to find a job of work.

v.

Here's how it's rigged in Perry, Oklahoma:
You gather outside the First National Bank before light.

You shoulder your way to the front of the line.
You wait for the flatbed drivers to arrive.

Reverse auction: I need five men to chop cotton.
Who will work longest for the least money?

And so the men undercut each other until
The pay is measured in pennies: climb on board.

Hoe handles pierce the hardest calluses
And you drain whatever you are into the red clay.

Maybe enough money for a bowl of chili
When you climb from the flatbed—maybe.

It's always gone too soon. Hunger gurgles at midnight.
Oklahoma: 1928, and it's the best that you can find.

Pull yourself up, boy, this is America. Think you know
Hard times? I can tell you all about hard times.

Cave With No Name

There is no wind. We drive around hills
thick with live oaks and mountain cedars.
Boerne, Texas, and a Klan rally is the news, so
we avoid the courthouse square. I feel pressure.

The man who owns the cave with no name
wears coveralls and an engineer's cap. A pink
scar seasons his face. His left eye is glass. He lifts
the rusted barbed wire, the cedar post. We trip
inside, following bulbs strung with braided cords.

Halfway down, the power dies. The press of darkness
sends me falling backward. I strike my head on limestone.
"I'll come for you," the man shouts. "Don't worry."
But for me it is no more than the comfort of cold stone,
the trickle of blood down my neck.

She reminds me: twenty years ago I folded what I had
and buried it in a different place. I could not stand
the unforgiving plains. Too much to see: grain elevators,
drive-in movies, oil derricks against the horizon.
Too much light. I traded it for the cool and the dark.

The eyeless man will never rescue us
in this black silence of only breathing.

Letter from Amarillo

Some absurd business trip, and
I'm staying in a death rattle motel
Just down from the AQHA,
Reading about Leonard Peltier when I can.

No sleep, the guy with whom I'm rooming
Rattles his sinuses all night, and I'm wasted.
Stumble down to the lobby of this place—someone
Had great plans for it, before the oil

And agriculture bust sent it to Chapter 11, to
Find my free breakfast: chunky cold scrambled
Eggs, cold toast, lukewarm coffee, tepid waiter.
I leave half of it behind, get more coffee,

Carry my styrofoam out to the breaking dawn,
Purple and blue fingers over orange. Someone is
Playing Jesus radio in the distance.
I settle against some iron rail, let my brain vibrate,

When in a heat dream a maroon Chevelle SS 396,
maybe a '69 model,
Primo muscle car, purrs into the back lot on new wide ovals,
White lettering. Doors open and out step four Comanches,
Squat horsemen, no problems scaling the folded front seat.

Faces painted black and white, carrying lances, replete
With fresh scalps, eyes electric brown, scaring me shitless:
Honey-eaters, they steal the horses from the trailer behind
The AQHA, mount bareback, rein silently away into a gallop

After the disappeared buffalo above Palo Duro.

Part II

My father was of the opinion that you earned what you got. Nothing was ever given to you . . . Even when we grew up, he was still tough, and he'd knock you on your ass if you were out of line. . .

— Sam Peckinpah

Homage to Don Meredith

The boy in a nowhere trailer watches
A screen gray as November's sky:
Here is a snowy image dropping back,
Here is a blurred uncolored rainbow,
Here is end zone impossibility –
Meredith to Hayes–
And across the room
The smeared-grease man in coveralls
Whoops, sloshing the Old Forester and Coke
In the jelly glass on his lap:
His mind is Cotton Bowl joy.

And for that instant
The bruising belt on a nail
Next to the shop door
Becomes innocent as licorice.
Work boots no longer shatter flesh.
Bone-hard backhands
That could roll you across the linoleum
Yield like feathers.

The boy looks up:
For once, a smile.

An Emptiness I Can't Raise

i.

I started in on *Zen and the Art of Motorcycle Maintenance* again last night. Damn it, I knew better, knew I'd drift back to the mid-1970s, knew I'd start thinking about you. Knew I'd ease away to something I thought I'd made peace with, but haven't. Christ, those were about the best times of my life.

Begin with the Beer House. You at your stool, Parliament cigarettes on the counter, a couple of empty Bud bottles, the plastic cup holding ice and Old Taylor and nothing else: your first serious drinking of the day. I sit woozy with beer and the darkness and the duskiness of the woman behind the bar.

I'm still young enough for acne, still young enough for the stomach lump when I think of my high school girlfriend, who dumped me. You, you're talking about teaching with Wendell Berry at the University of Kentucky, a story or two about Creeley, whom you also knew. My copy of Edward

Abbey on the bar, *Desert Solitaire*, and you're saying, yeah I remember a book by this guy I read years ago, *The Brave Cowboy*, made it into a movie with Kirk Douglas, hell of a movie. Abbey, yeah, wondered what happened to him. Then you're off to play shuffleboard with some carpet layers

before you come back and we talk about Dr. Johnson and melancholy and the poetry of Hank Williams. And all around me is this great *realness*, carpenters and university professors, ceiling sprayers and lawyers, drillers, dipshit students like me, women and men on the make, dope dealers:

a good air of the criminal here, Old T.B., possessor of a murder rap; his son, Young T.B., popped for selling cocaine. And mad ones, like Leroy. So now you're off lyrics and on to putting points and plugs on a small block Chevy engine. And I'm overcome by it all: this is life, heady life.

Or begin with a duck hunting trip, the sloughs around the Cimarron, the area where Karen Silkwood died, and you're drinking beer a half hour before dawn, whirring mystery ducks over our backs, divers, we know from the sound, but what kind? Eerie, the beating wings on air at this hour. Beer

smells as we huddle down in the blind made of broom weed, the decoys barely visible. The whir becomes a roar, almost, a time or two. But as the gray grows lighter, only our decoys bob in the water, with a coot, the same coot that has been in this muddy water for more than

a week. We leave, game bag empty; drained Bud cans rattle the back of your old red pickup. We rock up the pasture ruts. You want a tavern; we'll find one: Travel Inn (stagger out). You talk your dream of pheasant hunting in Nebraska. The camper, the whiskey, the skinned hens stewing.

Or begin with a night at your place, peppermint schnapps, how could you go from Old Taylor to this? A woman (not your wife) weeping in the kitchen. Banging guitars around with Leroy and me. Strumming, out of key, that saddest of songs, Johnny Cash's "I Still Miss Someone." How did we get here?

ii.

I know a story you never told me. You were a young man in Colorado, just beyond your wild-one stage. Heavy construction in Denver in summer to pay college bills. Picking up winos in Larimer Square (before yuppie renovation, when the square was still flophouse-Cassady country) and trucking them off to a building site. Working your way through those dark daytime joints, where the lights were always blue and the wine always sweet. Your nights passed with a young *chicana*. I never heard her name.

One night she wasn't home when you arrived. You asked her family: She is gone, she is out-of-town, she will not come back, *por favor*, do not bother her again. Not good enough, those explanations, for you. 1950s manhood wouldn't let you give up. You searched, found her at the house of a cousin, asked her what was wrong. It took awhile, then you learned. Missed her time. The doctor and the vomiting confirmed it. You didn't hesitate: I'll marry you. No, she said, no, because you don't want to marry me for who I am, just for what has happened. Cousin and two *pachuco* dudes (pegged pants, sharp shoes) showed up, threw your ass out of the house. You came back; they beat shit out of you. You returned once more, your soul bloodied, all you were turned inside out, and she was gone.

For years you tried to find her. No luck. A son, your blood, somewhere there in the Rockies, unfound. Or so went the story. Was this the explanation for everything? Or did it explain nothing? I wish we had talked about it. I know something about missing fathers and sons. I know something about emptiness. I know the mountains.

iii.

You arrive at my house for a party.
Drunk, no surprise, I guess. I hoped
for more. I want my friends to meet
this great scholar, this living novel.

I want them to know what you mean
to me. You tell a story about getting
crabs from a good girl back in college.
You ask the women to dance. You

come across a little too friendly. A couple
of my buddies, whose wives you've hit on,
take me aside. Do something, they say.
Or we'll beat the fuck out of him.

What am I supposed to do? Nothing, as
it turns out. You leave on your own,
drunk in your pickup. February winds
chill my house. You don't have long.

iv.

And I stayed away too long   secluded on a farm not far
from nowhere   trailer-house nightmare   always pangs
about not checking up on you, knowing the path you'd chosen
Thunderous spring and I go looking for you   at last

Him?
He's dead, didn't you hear?

No, I didn't

They tried to find me but I had successfully disappeared   I learn
it all second-hand   the drunken fall, the cracked skull, the loss
of blood
Cremation and burying the urn

beneath a favorite crepe myrtle   Someone sang
Dylan songs   I'm glad I missed it   Sunniest spring and
I hear Willie
Nelson sing about karma on the country radio
karma!   I want to cry but I can't   I never cry over lost
people
a shortcoming I confess   Still something settles over me

an emptiness I can't raise   too many singers for this moment

What I want is one broken baritone,
in a pickup,
in unrecovered mist.

Shooting Snooker at the Vencedora

These oil patch boys will peel you to bone!
Your father crows as he tangos from counter
To table, cue in hand. He breathes his whiskey
Spell over the red balls. *Snooker is the real*
Game! Even the khakied codgers bent over
Domino tables up front affirm with emphysema
Hacks. *Stroke it as you would a lady!* And
His break is sober as cardboard and perfect.
Pot the red, pot the colored, methodically
On this acre of baize, pockets tricky
An old lover's lips. The roughnecks
Hide their wallets, but the cheap blend-
Reddened eyes miss not a thing. They're had.
Half the wages of a West Texas morning tour
Will flutter into this old drunk's tremble
Before the evening's over. You've lived
This movie time and again and again.

An alley exit and a newly busted seal,
A stumble and you're in his arms, lifeguard
Rescue of a drowning boy as you both totter
To filthy asphalt. With streetlight eyes he demands:
Why do you never brag on me? You can't speak.

Three decades later the memory taste of cue-chalk
Dust and soiled felt paralyze your tongue. He never
Departs, not even in death. You study your own
Hands as they quiver and profess the drunk son's
Creed, dreaming of a Vencedora of your own,
Bone-peeled oil-patch boys to pay off the night.

Apology

My old man steps over to this worn-out
Datsun pickup I'm working on,
leans an arm onto the windshield, says:
It was how Dad done us: He was tough.

I look up. The old man's a battler. Scarred bald
head, result of a fuel tank fire; blind in one eye,
crippled by arthritis; high blood pressure flush.
A battler struggling to hang on.

He continues:

He used to be real hard on us, call you
every name in the book, make fun of you,
make you feel like you was stupid,
not worth anything.

So I never learned how to teach you boys
            the right way. I couldn't—

He shakes his head, steps away.

On the glass:
oil smudge where his hand died.

Someplace in Oregon (Father's Day)

He left something after all.

Cascade morning along the freeze line,
far away from everything I know—
he's in a package under my arm,
unclaimed ashes for five years until now.

I wade into mountain water up to my knees.
I lose my feet—firs high as Ferris wheels,
my mind rolling. I rip open the paper, pull
back the lid of the box, dump him into the river.

I'm alone but not really—Hells Angels on a smoke break
watch me. A gray heart blossoms in the water.
It holds against the current. I shake my soaked legs.
An Angel waves his hand: We battle this together.

Part III

Well, there are two kinds of women. There are women and then there's pussy. A woman is a partner. If you can go a certain distance by yourself, a good woman will triple it . . . Most of us marry pussy at one time or another.

—Sam Peckinpah

Like a lot of us, Sam had a lot of bad examples for how to treat women. I think Sam loved women, deeply—and was afraid of them.

—Kris Kristofferson

Flight Fear

We sleep in rooms apart.
I never hear her breathe.
Her hands are frozen.

Her feet fall numb.
She misses her cigarettes.
She drinks too much Scotch.

She no longer dreams.
I dream of snow and water.
I dream of women of sand.

I awake above the desert:
Flight 1532, crowded
With rodeo fantasy,

New hats and stiff jeans,
Snap of turquoise and silver
Against Coors Light cans.

(Somewhere she is alone
In her broadcast,
Unable to telephone.)

I see a train below:
How far? 20,000 feet?
Straight steel and diesel

Riding straight steel tracks
Across straight desert flats.
L.A. maybe? San Diego?

Fuselage turns sleeper car
And I curl in the berth,
Five beers still to go.

(Somewhere she lies
Dreamless in the cold,
Each breath unheard.)

"Drink up!" I say, and
Leroy, old ghost, joins in:
Liberation! Celebration!

On the rocking train.
And the desert dies
To our dirty stories.

And the plane flies
Along straight steel
Until it strikes California.

LAX: lights, security
Too much of both.
My head hurts.

I am lost, as usual.
Leroy vanished
A long time ago.

(Somewhere she reaches . . .)

Driving up Sepulveda,
Boulevard of gold images
Corroded to silver;

Dreamers faded
To dead faces
Hustling the street.

She once sang:
"You got to move."
But I lost her

To museum sleep,
To flight fear,
To suburban curbs.

Her memory:
an age spot.

At the Dobie Ranch

The last Paisano longhorn stumbles and dies.
No one knows what to do. Burial? Quick lime?
We call in experts. The answer, easy:
Let vultures do the job. So we watch.
Five days and we are down to hide and bone—
Black dreams slicing the autumn horizon.
We nail the horns to a live oak and waltz
To whiskey serenades in a collapsed house.

Now you check for life in darkness, cool sheets,
Slick pillows, light breeze. I remove your hand.
Everything fell with that steer. Suburbs hum
Their air-conditioned refrain. Developer engines
Fire up at dawn as buzzards complete their
Night work. And I lose again, spiked to the tree.

Letter from Port Aransas

Something unknowable within her rises,
and the sky grays. She withdraws.
I know I demand too much. The dawn
fishermen creak over board galleries,
the gulf beckoning. Soon we will
hear their motors over the two-note gulls.
Somewhere a tug rumbles. Her face is dreary
as the sky. I want to reach her, but
there is no touching her at these times.

Better days and dolphins hook channel waves
near the ferry landing. She swims with them,
snapshots for the tourists. I wrap myself
with her and smile. The tankers heave
our glitter stream. We kiss and live.
The dolphins carry us in the trashy gulf,
far away from ruined drilling platforms,
rusted shrimpers, and bloodless lovers.
We can breathe in the blue water.

Face Across a Crowded Restaurant Dining Room in Uvalde, Texas

No wrinkles then, hair blazing
into sandy embers in the moonlight

Filtered through the granite teeth
of Quartz Mountain. 1978 and

Atlanta Rhythm Section harmony
on the radio. You were never

Imaginary: Sigh of flame on my
neck, wine lips, taste of tears

On your cheek. Where did I
lose myself? Somewhere far

From that holy place. Your hand
on mine should have been my

Island in that seal-less place. Lightning
west on the Kiowa plain. I should

Have swallowed it, held it an eternity,
flashed it through my pores, sang it.

I see you now, the lightning frozen
into stone long ago, discarded. Your

Hair is roadside slush. Your face
scored like those sharp boulders.

Our eyes lock. I flutter. But
you—

Look down at the guacamole plate,
reaching for the old man beside you.

Of course. Pretending is the
only thing now. I'm old too.

Outside the night is cold,
breathless. Stars painted

Over. I touch the door, ponder
my return as the dead dome shatters.

Above Love: 1971

Fourteen years of ice-burned tears
blur dying houses in a dying town
and here you are: Jane Ann's
living room and all is winter except

her smile. She plays her big sister's
copy of Ten Years After (Cricklewood
Green) and you ache to love like a man
most of the time, but not now. You

need her more than love. You need
her eyes bright and brown while sleet
snaps the windows and no one knows
you're not at home. You're glad

she's on the couch and you're on the chair;
that's perfect for now. Alvin Lee's
fingers probe 50,000 miles beneath
your brain, and it's all right. You forget

death and the cold. She tilts her head
and you are not alone. (Four decades
later, you'll remember her and
that stricken afternoon, grateful for

gifts above love.) The sleet conjures rain
and, at last, you stumble out to
cellophane ice and gravel, frozen grass
crunching below your boots. Love like

a man—oh sure: Rooms ahead loom black
and empty and you'll be abandoned
forever. But you'll cradle her light in the
cup of your palms for the rest of the road

and post it in blank air, soaring
as you slide under your own wind.

Momento: Quartz Mountain

Irrigation persists. Piercing night
Are bones of the drowned town
As the reservoir quenches soybean
Fields. You battle mosquitoes

On the desert shore, granite ghosts
Hiding a full moon. Someone has painted
"Have YOU Been Washed In The Blood
Of The LAMB?"—white on red stone.

Her hips are firm as soybean earth.
Her eyes are dark as yesterday's music.
Her lips and tongue taste of beer.
Her hair smells of weed and bug spray.

She laughs as transport planes vulture
Their way to Altus Air Force Base. She
Rolls another joint and says she's the best
Actress Lubbock will ever produce.

You know she's here with a friend.

Boats banned because of the drowned town.
What water there is drinks the light. You
Part the sleeping bag, darkness out of darkness.
She is wetter than the lake. And you could

Drown yourself tonight as she swallows you,
Your bones piercing night. Her friend declines
Your rescue. Just beer and weed and bug spray
And pussy in the lamb's blood shadow.

You carry her bruises.

When the Depression Flies

Steam wings away from the first
cold water of the fall. We drive slowly
across the bridge. We've gone too fast
before. On the radio: "Everything

is going to be all right. Oh yeah." When
the depression lifts—wood smoke memories
and the scent of strawberry from a
1972 letter, but no questions.

Just rest and calm. The car rolls onward
through the growl of Muddy Waters:
glass on flat-wound strings. Used up
amplifier. Someone out of tune, no matter.

When the depression flies, she is rye grass
in autumn, low clouds, and slow rolling.

Other than Love

I awake in darkness, sweating.
I swim in lakes that have never
known fish. I climb fruitless trees.
I find roses that have no color,
smell of nothing, threaten no thorns.

I awake in darkness, sweating.
I understand now. The moon is flesh.

For a Woman I Once Knew

Sometimes I hear the old songs all day:
Mewl of steel guitar behind fire's
Too familiar lament, a lonesome fiddle.
Sometimes it's George Jones from the

Early '60s and the bite of a saw into
Green wood, the wind over the chimney.
The beer foam clings to my lips.
This tavern is nearly dark, nearly deserted:

No windows, the only light from
The jukebox glow. It is winter.
The forms here once were human.
I am this tavern. I am wasted and young.

You came at the perfect moment,
Sun and clear skies as the last song died.

At Louie Mueller's

One day I sat in Louie Mueller's old place
down in Taylor. Drinking Lone Star—
none of that yuppie Bock crap—watching
Baylor and TCU play football on a woebegone
portable TV, eating barbecue. Thinking of her,
and I didn't even know her yet. Thinking,
she'd give me hell for all this grease and beer;
thinking, then she'd say it's all right: You have
to every once in a while. Hell of a thing, because
I'd never spoken to her, just seen her face,
seen her smile. Wasn't even sure if I'd could
recall her name, but that smile: It was forever.

I don't want you think this was obsession
or anything. It wasn't. Instead:

It was Louie Mueller's, that smoky gymnasium of a
barbecue joint; it was the live oaks and wildflowers
and river bottom pecans and a crackly *norteño* AM station
on the pickup radio; it was a sky that seemed too big
for itself, sometimes was too big for itself. All this, and
her smile. I sensed, somehow, they spelled

all that I ever would become.

Light

Light: a face flame, words
spoken in clear, warm rooms—

moteless shaft through clean windows
to make my body electricity.

She is light.

She breaks at dawn to heal me.
She draws me to her at dusk.

I slid blind for decades.
I see now in her glow.

We are light.

Flesh and Necessity

You crave lightning and storm wind.
You need thirsty skin to heal
Unforgiven yesterdays. You require
Mountain wailing, old as whiskey itself.
Sometimes you collapse inside yourself,
Unsatisfied—unable to say why.
Sometimes you shiver in summer,
Dark above sunlight—unable to see why.

But everything is complete
When she smiles with her eyes.
She feeds you her lips and you
Possess more than can be owned.
Her gift is flesh and necessity:
You need her to get by.

Hayloft Apartment

The apartment started out
As a carriage house hayloft
That was ninety years earlier

When I moved in
I paid $65 a month
For no air-conditioning
And nickel-thick gaps
Between floor planks

Sometimes Sharon called
At five in the morning
And I listened to her tears
For an hour or two
Other times she parked
Her red VW in the alley
And came upstairs
To drill the cast iron bed
Into the pine decking
Her wet reminders everywhere

Once a lightning strike
Kicked me from the sheets
That was during May
Sharon was losing herself
Somewhere

I remember late winter days
Alone behind steamed glass
Snow outside shin deep and I'd think
About Sharon while listening
To Tonight's the Night
By then she had married a TV producer
Or a man from Vietnam
I was never sure
Neil Young's "New Mama"
Played over and over
As I stared at the frozen alley

Finally I decided to wed myself
A woman I never really knew
Sharon was long gone by then
I coated everything
With eggshell white
And gave the landlady
My last rent check
No one ever painted
Before me, the landlady said

I smiled and rolled away
From the hayloft apartment
A year later it burned
My eggshell white
And Sharon's stains
Erased by flame.

Hidden in Blackjacks

Sometimes I recall a house hidden in blackjacks— Kate Flaherty
sophisticated
Beyond my reckoning—a woman named Libby who seldom
wore under-
Wear in summer—Frank out back watering marijuana he never
smoked and
I—callow as the pale green spider under the redwood deck.
Pat insisted on side two Sweetheart of the Rodeo above all other
music—
I loved those arts girls before they turned to law and Volvos—
And I loved the Byrds with Gram Parsons—I cooked chili for
everyone
And always got it too *picante*—I made everything too *picante*
then.
My wife suffered all that never complaining—I complained
plenty
About everything I failed to be—everything I believe I merited—
Even when the sky was blue beyond blue and people professed
Love I demanded more—I wished I wrote "Hickory Wind" for
one.
I wished my wife was more like Pat—my wife professed a fancy
for Boston,
The rock group—for Christ's sake—she hated my love of Merle
Haggard
And raised eyebrows every time Sweetheart of Rodeo played but
I was
Certain of what I deserved—and did not deserve how I
undersold myself.
So I wound up with the Boston woman so uncomplicated.

Now I wish I could call her say forgive me and somehow make
her world little more violet but it's too late and the real
problem was walking
In a door best left closed to begin with—one I took because I
thought
It was the only door available for me (now I kick in doors when I
can).
Explanations? Maybe I know one or two—I can talk about the
carnie cowboy

Who ran away or never was or whatever and about a sloppy
grackle
Nest of denials in a hardass town known for treasuring liars but
why?
What's done is swallowed and digested and nothing changes
that.
Besides these years later I understand Pat was just another
woman and that house
Hidden in blackjacks is falling apart if it's even still standing at
all
And Libby is past her prime and wears underwear and my beard
is white
And this drama's culprits are dying or dead and sorry repairs
nothing.

I haven't cooked chili in years.

Football Poem

Leaving Memorial Stadium in broken sunlight
The game out of hand, Colorado down three
Touchdowns.

Aroma of car exhaust and barbecue.
First dreams of a blonde in a red sweater.
One smile

Twenty-five years ago in a blue VW.
She's dead now—dead before this team
Was born.

My knees ache, autumn approaches.
It's peaceful here on Red River, no one moving.
Her name

Was Paula, her hand tiny on mine:
I remember that, remember thinking
No way

Could I see her finger on the trigger,
Much too delicate for that.
The crowd

Roaring behind me, another score?
An old hippie smoking dope, alone
Gray hair

Like dead weeds on his shoulders.
Someone plays Joni Mitchell from
Somewhere.

She loved Joni Mitchell, electric piano,
Sad songs, tiny fingers pale against black
Vinyl,

Pale on cold blue steel, alone that night
A thousand football games ago. Celebration
And songs

She never heard, eyes as blue as the VW.
Love and tears in that cramped space,
Joni

On the eight-track, tears down her cheek
As it touched mine, child fingers
Reaching

To brush them away. Fire the coach, bench the
Quarterback. I've heard it until my brain bleeds.
Her lips

Tasted like green apple candy. Her eyelashes tickled
My tear-wet cheek, my hand inside the red sweater.
She sighed.

I wad up the football program. A long time ago
Suicide word at a different game. I held my head
Dry-eyed.

At the Marfa Mystery Lights Viewing Area

We secede from ourselves, burrow beneath
The broken tortoise shell of the sky.
For these moments we don tourist souls,
Ignoring clogged restroom stench and
Plastic littered across the Chihuahuan floor,
Peering out at the far edge of nothing.

We spy four gold orbs in the southwest sky,
Then a fifth, scintillating much higher,
Then a sixth and then a seventh.
A few frozen in the desert heat.
Two waltzing as awkwardly
As finished lovers on a last date.

Ghost lights.

Ain't nothing but cars on some old highway,
Cackles a beery West Texas honey.

Wait til you see one shoot half way across the moon,
Replies her tattooed boyfriend in the Toby Keith tank top:
I seen it. It can happen.

She says: *I can tear right out of here too.*

When you aren't looking, I tear right out myself,
Leaving you behind with the scattered trash.
I vault the fence, praying for rattlesnakes.
I run Mitchell Flat maybe three miles before I stop,
My breath a freight train in the distance,
My heart open to gilded globes to spirit me away.

But there are only mesquites
And blue pools of nothing.

Part IV

I think they might have been not cruel but mean to Sam . . . We were taught not to show our feelings . . . Sam was not given leeway to cry or to be hurt . . . Sam had a very soft sweet side to him, a tender side to him . . . Trying to live up to being a tough guy, it was difficult for Sam. If he'd been left on his own, he would have been more creative . . .

—Fern Lea Peter, Peckinpah's Sister

We Were Hippies Once

We were hippies once, and the water slap
Of Lake Tenkiller kept time to out-of-tune
Guitars and racked harmonicas. Somewhere
A fishing boat buzzed as our weed smoke
Drifted to black skeleton trees past the dock.
That night you laughed and gargled Coors
And said no one should treat you that way.
Then it was Neil Young and sand cowgirls.

Tonight on the phone your voice crumples
As we condone pacemakers and defibrillation.
Remember Mother's Rock Shop? The Paseo?
Oklahoma City, 1970? How did our time die?
You know, I still dream that dark lake water.
We were hippies once, drenched yet breathing.

Bard in Red River

And what do we know of passion?
His eyes ask that as he sits
In the wooden booth, plastic
Checked tablecloth, red bled to pink,
Soul-patch like Satan, *imperial* like
A conquistador breathing Comanche
Dust. Bald but for fringe embracing
His collar. He's an unusual one,
The waitress tells us, but smarter
Than he looks, smarter than most.

But I don't trust those *molé*-colored pupils.

They yawn like omens plastered
Against the loaf of his face.
Try the barbecue chicken, hon,
The waitress implores and I do.

(—For this two days of food
Poisoning in Taos, revived only
When I down two Lotaburgers
During a thunderstorm—)

He steps toward us, muttering,
Pretty crappy excuse for a day,
Ain't it? Rattling baritone
Like Waylon Jennings. Just
Get in from Lubbock? I ask.
He shudders, a wet dog, then
Says: Wedding is great Juno's crown,
O blessed bond of board and bed!

(Why couldn't we accept my wreckage?)

He says: What are you made of?
You'll not fight nor fly.

And he is right.

I study your red tear swell
Here in these unforgiving mountains
And collapse into the sunset.

The Last Rehearsal

Here we are in the disease
Of Oklahoma, 1972, slate sky
And dead trees—

Huddled by the gas fire
Wind ahowl outside
The grease hair wino

Asks for the guru song
One more time—
You wrote it, you sing it

When it's sung at all—
That and a song about Jesus
Like a latter day Byrd

In a sweet smelling
Rent house on Broad Street
But your lips are cracked

You don't feel like singing—
D.K. is handling that
And a red B.B. King guitar—

Besides you don't know
This wino at all—
D.K. offers a mescaline tab

Wrapped in aluminum foil
The color of his eyes—
But you say no and hope

You're never cornered again—
D.K. shrugs, sails on alone
The wino waving

From the dry living room pier.

Knoxville Allergies

i.

Here we see the house where Agee
Dreamed hissing lawns and falling men.
You fight back vomiting as towers spin
Even though you've had nothing to drink.
Sometimes you climb into yourself
To touch the clogged passes, soothe
The once exploded drums. But nothing
Can ease this disruption. Knoxville
Is the worst for allergies, you're told,
And you ingest those words and nod,
Praying the acid voids as you peer up
At the football temple, biggest in the South,
Dwarfing Agee's place, dwarfing Confederate
Ghosts, dwarfing *Thunder Road* memories:
Beacon Drive In, 1962, a different place—
You don't look so good, you hear, as forest
Dogwoods and God knows what else assault.

No, I'm not well, you concur. You handle
Dinner and conversation, and then it's back
To a mold-scented motel—You're in luck!
The Mary Kay convention is in town! the clerk
Enthuses—and you smile and manage a nod
Though the machete pain across your forehead
Never breaks. In the sweat bed Agee's ghost
Speaks, reminding you of love that ended
Short of itself. Agee, did you follow
Vols football? No, probably you did not,
Sewanee snob that you became, dead
Too soon for Johnny Majors; and too soon
For *Thunder Road* (which you surely
Would have hated). Agee, did you suffer
From these mountain allergies? No,
You must have been immune, all that
Time with your ears on the cut grass
Sprinkler singing above you.

ii.

I awaken, head throbbing so much
My pillow vibrates. I've swallowed
More than I can, so I pad down dim hallways
Barefoot in cowboy pajamas,
Returning with ice I dump on the sham.
I freeze my face yet the room still spins
And Episcopal hymns dance on my lips
But Agee is drunk, can't sing harmony
On this, my trip to make homage, of a sort.
Liturgy and incense and holy water—
High church rites I scarcely remember:

In Agee there is no east or west,
In Him no north or south, just crucifixion
On the whiskey bottle, destroyed heart
At age forty-five, yet he tended love
Better than I, world without end, amen.
So I'm left with Knoxville allergies
As the Imus story plays out on cable news
And the Mary Kay conventioneers check
For hail damage to pink Cadillacs
And pollen sifts through 1928 Prayer Books.

iii.

Hear, O Agee, my supplications:
Let me breathe again.
Let me see geese drift over the river.
Let me open myself to love.
Let me be forgiven.
Let me see *Thunder Road* and *Night of the Hunter*
    on a drive-in twin bill.
Let me canoe once more.
Let me weep over lost trains.
Let me pluck "Black Mountain Rag."
Let me run like Johnny Majors.
Let me douse this fever and fly forever sideways
    from this poisoned swirl:

Redeemed.

Only Eagles Song You Ever Liked, Sort of, and Why

And the sweat of still nineteen years old
In a rumbling Chrysler, North May Avenue,
Oklahoma City, driving out to the red-lit
Broadcast tower district and the vacuum beyond,
Summer 1975, and you've had enough of beer and smoke.

Instead—
Her center is fragrance on your fingers still,
Her other perfume sweet on your collar and lips,
Soaring here on the trafficless four-lane:
This is everything, *everything*, and every last thing—

And the new song blares the FM radio,
One of these nights,
Her devil's daughter breath mingled in dead wind
At your back, and you pray you'll hold that black road
Past its end, knowing you'll never taste her again.

Sour Rain

The music I love hums
Sorrow beyond sad, disturbing
Friends and ex-spouses

Who e-mail their worry.
The music I love is sour rain
Lost in February gray.

Scratchy black preachers
On Depression-era 78s,
That speaks to me—

And straw-thin country crooners,
Pissed off and out-of-tune,
Knife threats, mean women.

T-Model Ford cranked up now—
Baby, call to your daddy,
And I'll testify to the truth.

Listen and stay dry.
We all walk the storm.
This is the best way.

Nebraska Radio Station Fire

An answer must glow beneath these ashes
But who can detect that heat? Winds down
From Belle Fourche, South Dakota, ice
The Sand Hill Country. We have no sticks
To poke what remains. Day is night dark,
Almost, and we can't stay long. The obit
Fluttered away long ago. Why did we marry?

You've had enough, stomp back to the car.
I stay to kick the frozen, fire-black bricks
For a while longer in the crippled light.
I decline admitting we've arrived
At the wrong place. But you will proclaim it
For eight hundred miles to every
Silo and corner post fouling the horizon.

Detour apologies salve nobody, I'm certain.
So I brick kick, refuse to glance over my shoulder.
We are frozen by prairie gales blowing nothing.

Brothers

i.

First: hissing ventilator,
too hot in ICU—never mind the coldest
winter on record outside: sad
Dallas Christmas decorations
against a battleship sky. My brother,
yet not my brother, IVs,
iodine smears on his chest. Eyes of a dying
animal when they open.

Soul of a dying animal
when it opens.

ii.

I touch him. The foundation
of a man is all that remains. Blood and cold
skin and bones.

I don't know how much you know
about your brother's condition—
the head ICU nurse is saying—
but he has something like pneumonia
though not really pneumonia.

That's all we can say, orders
he gave the doctor, the hospital. . .

And secret decades demand release
into that frozen sky.

iii.

The wind cries. I hear traffic. Somewhere
a child sings "Jingle Bells."
I know nothing.
I know everything.

Here is his mother, not
my mother. She embraces me.
More than thirty years and we've never
touched. Never had need to
touch. Here is his sister, not
my sister . . . more than thirty years. . .

My heart dies in the hospital cafeteria,
chicken and rice gray as the sky outside.

You've got to call them—she is saying—
they'll listen to you, never to me. . .

iv.

And so I call. My mother, not his, on the phone.
Four hours on the Interstate if they
come.

You better come

They arrive. The old man, a little
boy lost in snow. My mother,
curling a lip at his mother.

We cannot speak..

v.

I know what it is, cannot tell
anyone the truth.
Always the story in my family.

Always so much easier to pretend.

I expect death before daybreak.
But he survives. Survives through Christmas,
sees the new year
through eyes clamped shut.

vi.

Then the new year dies for him.
Before it really begins.
A phone call for me at six in the morning.

I remember that dawn: bluebirds on spent bermuda.

vii.

And that bright day so long ago
comes to me. We laugh over

a joint. Confession time
but not really.

He said:
I always thought you knew how I am.

Laughing again, easy. He made
fun of me for liking Willie Nelson.

Everything was glass between us
after that:

Dallas 'burbs, 1982.

viii.

I see him now in repose against the satin.
He is
a photo of an Auschwitz victim in the snow-mud.
I say to the undertaker—
tell me the precise cause of death?

I'm so
relieved you asked. I don't think your dad
knows yet, and he needs to know . . . before he sees it
as words on paper.

ten thousand storm troopers walk the streets of my
home town this night. Ten thousand ready
to hack us all to pieces. String us up
with piano wire.

My mother is tranquilized.

Still I tell her:
no more time
to put it off.

She pauses over sheets, continues
but not a word splits her lips.

ix.

My other stepbrother is drunk, too alive.
The old man is lost
in 1950s West Texas, red-eyed,
convinced he could have
done something if only he'd known.

Nothing would
change anything, I want to tell him.

Nothing but glass and light.

But I remain quiet, the family way,

aching for anything to break.

x.

Burial next day, split open Oklahoma red clay.
Campbellite preacher, cedars the only green.
Push of wind, dead grass,
Oklahoma never changes. I'm lost.

I fuck up my job as pallbearer, turn the wrong way.
But it's to be expected: I am the family fuck up.

My dead heart lies in the box with him
though I don't know it yet.
Everything ends for me at that moment.
Nearly five years pass before I understand.

My stepbrother, *our brother*, is dirt.
Whatever became
from the death of us
grows in that dirt.

Part V

Of all the whores I've been with. . .I've failed to end up in some kind of warm personal relationship with only about ten percent. I've lived with some good whores.

—Sam Peckinpah

Thirty-eight Truths About Whores

1.
They euphemize only when describing what they are.

2.
They are all broken, but no more so than you or I.

3.
They pray more often than you think, though they really
do not believe in God.

4.
They believe the Internet has been a godsend for their business.

5.
They believe the Internet has made their business
a thousand times more dangerous.

6.
They eventually tell their mothers, who surprise them
by understanding.

7.
They are never truly bisexual.

8.
They loathe hairspray and mousse.

9.
They comprehend Buddhism.

10.
They believe everyone else's addiction is worse than theirs.

11.
They socialize with each other.

12.
They protect each other.

13.
They resent each other.

14.
They never have hearts of pure gold.

15.
They hate clients under thirty, particularly if they work in high-tech.

16.
They accept the reality that most of their clients will be under thirty and work in high-tech.

17.
They favor odd musical instruments, like metal clarinets.

18.
They drive woebegone cars.

19.
They prefer simile to metaphor.

20.
They read more than most people.

21.
They contemplate becoming roller derby girls.

22.
They have no feelings one way or the other about thunderstorms.

23.
They are perplexed by anyone who has ever considered becoming a cop.

24.
They all have thought about writing a book. They never get started on it, though.

25.
They respect Jehovah's Witnesses.

26.
They never feel lost; they never feel found.

27.
They never paint their nails for themselves.

28.
They don't like watching TV but watch it anyway.

29.
They know some karma debts are too great to repay.

30.
They like the Stones more than the Beatles but really prefer jazz and string quartets.

31.
They never drink Pepsi.

32.
They are just like your wife in every way.

33.
They are different from your wife in every way.

34.
They are certain they have lived a thousand lives
before this one.

35.
They never tell their fathers; most don't even speak to their
fathers.

36.
They do not like the color orange.

37.
They always feel shame when they cry.

38.
They bleed as much as anyone, even when they're not cut.

Part VI

I used to go to his office with a couple of guys a whole bunch of us who smoked grass, a tight-knit group. We were all closet smokers and Sam was one of us. Steve McQueen too, later on. Sam was one of the hip guys around. So we'd visit him and smoke a joint in his office or walk around the lot smoking a joint. He didn't say a hell of a lot.

—Dennis Hopper

Dennis Hopper

(For Roxie Powell and Charles Plymell and the Kansas Uprising)

i.

Dennis Hopper wore
A dusk-blue shirt
With a faded jean jacket
During those Taos days.

We saw him bearded.
He looked best clean-shaved.

Dennis Hopper said he liked
The Doors' "Soul Kitchen."
We once heard him whistling.
It was "Old Susannah."

No one cried for him alive.
He made crying impossible.

ii.

Dennis Hopper walked
Naked down a street
In Las Alamos. He said
It was an artistic statement.

He slept clothed on the grass
At J. Frank Dobie's old ranch.

Dennis Hopper fretted over Texas.
In Marfa, Rock Hudson's room
Was much larger than his.
Liz had a whole house to herself.

Dennis lay on a cast-iron bed
As Mexican wind blew over him.

iii.

Dennis Hopper painted
But favored the camera.
He sat for Andy Warhol in New York
But Marfa never left his mind.

His lips became granite bluffs—
His eyebrows, Wenders highways.

Dennis Hopper eventually played golf
And voted for Ronald Reagan.
He studied Henry Hathaway,
The director he hated most.

John Wayne saved his career:
Duke and Dennis, best buddies.

iv.

Dennis Hopper could sit a horse proper.
John Wayne always rode like a pilgrim.
John Wayne collected kachinas.
Dennis Hopper became one.

He tried singing with Johnny Cash.
He was better reciting Kipling.

Dennis Hopper filmed in Peru
Because the blow was the best.
Real cowboys, fake Indians.
Fake cowboys, real Indians.

Movie cameras fashioned of straw—
Stones, clubs, bullets of blood.

v.

Dennis Hopper guessed Duke
Never saw The Last Movie.
But John Wayne always laughed
At his Natalie Wood stories.

Hollywood champagne bath,
Her pussy burning afterward.

Dennis Hopper loved that one.
John Wayne liked it too.
Duke told it to John Ford.
Ford thought Dennis was a sot.

He might have fibbed that tale.
He could lie like false spring.

vi.

Dennis Hopper never gave
Terry Southern his due.
Dennis Hopper was darker
Than Peter Fonda ever was.

Yes, Wyatt was too too pale.
Billy was the color of soil.

Dennis Hopper grew black forms
Of ugly in the Sangre de Cristos.
Rumors spread of cauldrons
Of animal blood, of gunpowder:

Billy the Kid with Jesus hair
And Pancho Villa's mustache.

vii.

Dennis Hopper rode dirt bikes.
He couldn't mechanic worth a flip.
He also performed Harley ballets
At twenty-five miles per hour.

He married and divorced.
He played golf with Willie Nelson.

Dennis Hopper retreated to L.A.
He lived in a Venice compound.
Dryer lint traps mystified him.
He watched the NFL on TV.

But he never could leave Taos behind.
Autumn aspens flamed behind his eyes.

viii.

Dennis Hopper breathed tractor gas
To get stoned in Dodge City.
Pancho Villa died in Hidalgo del Parral.
Villa did not fake it and flee to Kansas.

Pancho Villa did not farm outside
Dodge City until an unripened old age.

Dennis Hopper was not Villa's secret son,
Born in 1936 while nuns planed doors.
Dennis' blood and Villa's blood
Ran together, but not in Kansas.

Now Dodge City is full of Mexicans.
Maybe Pancho Villa won after all.

ix.

Dennis Hopper never slaughtered
Steers at a packing plant—
A fine Dodge City tradition.
He bought outskirts tomato plants

At the Piggly Wiggly grocery store
When he visited in the 1980s.

Dennis Hopper inspected the truck
I drove and my broken ankle cast.
"Man," he said, "that takes courage."
He caressed the truck's leaking freeze plug.

He stood close to dying and knew it.
He spoke of the Clutters and Holcomb.

x.

Dennis Hopper skated back into life
And astonished everyone. He never
Refused a movie role and smoked
Cigars. He acted too much time and again:

Blue Velvet and Speed were overrated.
He was fine in Hoosiers and River's Edge.

Dennis Hopper knew to die in L.A.
But save the big adios for New Mexico,
Jack and Peter and Dean and Val all there—
White gloves, pine box, *Jesús Nazereno* dirt.

We mourned on Marfa streets, air dust
Swirling the Hotel Paisano, 527 miles below,

Wild born tears at last.

Part VII

I don't punch people anymore. My right hand's turned to mush. I'm getting too old for that . . . Basically, violence itself is stupid.

—Sam Peckinpah

Thirty-seven Boxing Haiku

1.
her eyes—swollen plums
heavy bag creaks on steel chain
her face—ripped cow hide

2.
round bell falls from wall
duct tape and it rings again
no religion here

3.
old men always watch
lean on blood spattered apron
still boxing courage

4.
kids slant-eyed, cocky
they lie about running miles
last only two rounds

5.
fight posters yellow
injury, not sun, on walls
winner pisses blood

6.
pissing blood again
filthy bowl in dark quarters
you know you're alive

7.
hand wraps wear out fast
Patterson sparred without them
knuckles turn to rust

8.
jump rope while hungry
lesson from Johnny Casas
sweating sustains you

9.
boxing movies fail
Rocky is the worst of them
come breathe the real world

10.
you know you're screwed
managers swallow fighters
promoters are worse

11.
they dream of Foreman
TV pitches, big money
unreachable door

12.
thirst garrotes your will
still you throw down for five rounds
August in Texas

13.
sometimes there is shame
mother will not watch her fight
brown shadow absent

14.
always veil yourself
coveralls and combat boots
roadwork before dawn

15.
mirror stare-down drill
motherfucker, i'll kill you
boring theater

16.
he fucks her, that's why
management question answer
Houston, Texas gym

17.
caterpillar crawl
boxer inches down the ropes
knees collapsing soon

18.
New York shit don't stink
promotion question answer
Austin, Texas gym

19.
San Antonio
dirtiest fighters around
forget Mexico

20.
casino boxing
lesson Oklahoma-learned
always get paid cash

21.
round girls—TECATE
on their ass—rate more applause
than the used up champ

22.
morning speed bag dies
two faces—Black, Mexican:
don't trust white women

23.
Australian lightweight
pants on the steps—his sister
burned off his tattoos

24.
boxer pounds truck tire
with Home Depot sledge hammer
the sky melts the sun

25.
we wave red flags here
stand and chant in *español*
champ fades on the stool

26.
no words for losing
cell phone silent—no doorbells
ticket stub—no dreams

27.
scar tissue blossoms
those eyes glowed beautiful
black Everlast gloves

28.
training in Texas
feet on fire before dawn
shooting star gone blue

29.
matchmaker in shades
stacks the take in fresh twenties
pit bull chained outside

30.
sports bra discarded
she gives tomorrow no weight
van slips-slips, fades-fades

31.
her manager frets
phone call: no fucking tonight
revenge is Sixth Street

32.
one pound above weight
so you sun-walk, spit in cup
climb naked on scales

33.
eight weeks, no orgasms
nights move like slow gravel trucks
we are old school here

34.
fight night brings out tits
who's heard of Niño Valdes?
glitter gap matters

35.
record: 0-8
why does he have a license?
never once knocked down

36.
homeless man mumbles
red sky—Creedence—God's bounty—
broken stick in ring

37.
boxer lives in gym
sleeping bag in ring, midnight
mother: Juárez dream

Lesson in Boxing

Never retreat from a punch:
Anticipate, slip or fade.
Then pivot and attack.

Her eyes pool-blue,
Her lips winter-dried,
Her goodbye on a Sunday.

My whiskers fell white.

Part VIII

Now the people who are really tough cats are the boys on the rodeo circuit. I mean I ain't that tough. I've tried it, but I just got the shit kicked out of me. I did it twice.

—Sam Peckinpah

Pink, Oklahoma: 1976

Axiom from the age of Gerald Ford:
Country singers prefer their Madonnas
In pink house-trailers off State Highway 9

Beyond Lake Thunderbird. I remember
Enchiladas scalded in chili gravy
And served in bird-bath plates, blistering all

Who touched them barehanded. I remember
Bearded truck drivers growling at braless
Modern dancers huddled with false poets

In overalls. I remember no songs
Except "Hotel California" and
"The Pretender" from Chevy radios,

Parking lot tunes, thin as 3.2 beer.
I preferred Merle Haggard, even then.
So too the truck drivers and dancers.

I wanted to ride like a *vaquero*
We all did during those misshelved years.
So we paused before the pink Madonna,

In the pink trailer, in the town of Pink,
And uttered pink rosary forgeries
While craving Mexican beer and thunder.

Quitters Paradise

I specialize in quitting. I know busted gates,
Filed gears, drooped power lines, stolen Bibles,
Rusted slots. You want to step aside, come see me:
Bring a moon smudged by thunderheads
And I'll tell you how it was, Ponca City, 1987,
How easy to glide bat-winged through the refinery

Blur to something reborn. Or Tulsa, 1989—best
Place yet, still I walked. You catch my current.
Grow a beard, paint your ears, tongue new accents
And you're done. Don't ask about love. I know only
Highway mileage markers, abandoned drive-in
Theaters, tire-fire mountains, Johnson grass ditches.

I talked to Billy Joe Shaver one August in a half empty
Barbecue joint. His advice: Sing only songs
You write yourself, then you never have to croon
"Borrowed Angel" to some drunk two tables back.
He winked and shook my hand with his missing fingers,
Then hooked it to climb the parking lot billboard.

So I rise to warn you I'm filled by my own symphonies.
I leave nothing in my pockets, sometimes skip airports
To crash runways I pave myself, too fast to give up
Every cool bed I've ever known. Touch your palm
To mine if you're ready to embrace this quitter's
Paradise. Roar with me and we'll disband asphalt,

Shatter concrete, swallow steel, peel this roadway,
Howl this refrain: Cowboys know how to run away.

National Finals Poem

i.
R.J. rode one more good lick, hit the Finals,
Oklahoma City, 1974—way too old for this shit,
Yet here he was. Drew a Hereford Brahma cross,
No Tornado, but one spinning son of a bitch.

R.J. played pitch with Freckles Brown the day
Before, Holiday Inn, private club in that time
Ahead of liquor by the drink. R.J. needed
Freckles' eyes; Freckles understood. Play him

Like some white mouse, Freckles grinned.
You have life insurance? Doubled it?
His teeth illegal ice cubes. He won the hand,
Raked R.J.'s dollars, then said, serious

As tequila: He'll explode to the left,
Whipsnap you back to the right, then
Drill your ass left again, horns dirt level,
And that bull will kill you if he dreams it.

Remember that—

ii.
R.J. squints fluorescents at Mercy Hospital
Two days later, tied to the bed, bandage
Wad where his left leg used to hang
And decides he should never have allowed

His hair to drift to his shoulders, not here,
Not in cowboy superstition. What else? Maybe
He ate chicken. Maybe he hurled his hat
On a bed. Maybe he donned yellow. Maybe

He laundered both mud and luck. Who
Could say? Morphine throbs and snow
Outside—they're his rodeo for today.
He recollects magpie visions and white water

Back home in Prescott.

Cheyenne Panic (Homage to Harry Dean Stanton)

You know one thing:
Open can swallow you whole
And this morning it happens
Here among the grass swales.

You've lost your breathing.
You've lost your wheel fingers.
You flee the highway
And dive the barbed wire.

Awake in the open country
You hear dead cattle sighs
From the 1887 blizzards
And shudder rodeo dreams.

Later you see a man
Who might be your father
At the rough stock chutes.
He rejects your call.

Rain, bad air-conditioning
And you're ready
For this show to end
With bull-rider flourish.

But it's never that way,
No risk of death,
No awestruck crowds,
Just you alone, always,

No trophy saddles,
No pastel buckle bunnies,
Just a truck stop motel
With a heart-free café.

You return to the Interstate
And plow the purple night.

Her Passion (Homage to Warren Oates)

Mexican paintings of martyrs
Are her obsession. And why not?
She climbs the cross ten times a day
To bleed in her own stigmata.

I drink sotol and mind my eyes.
Winter crawls into her shadow.
                    —I understand:
I once recited liturgy
Before I became a cowboy.

But I cannot abide one more
Crucifixion in our bedroom.
I have had enough of cedar,
Pine, and cypress—and vinegar . . .

I will ride to Ojinaga
At midnight, inhale half a moon,
Hitch my horse to the house of joy,
And wallow in *putas* until dawn,

Then wake, *la frontera* in haze,
Her relics vanquished by my stones.

Part IX

I'm a pretty good hunter and spearfisherman and a lousy skier, and a lousy surfer, but I'm up and on it.

—Sam Peckinpah

Letter to a Friend Long Dead

Bill, please find enclosed a 3x5 print
of Rainy Mountain.
I hope this will make up for the time we meant
to look for it,
but lost it.

The sky really is about that shade of blue,
dying cornflowers this time of year.
The grass is more like the moon on a clouded night.
The stones are less than flesh.

Behind this photo
you can spot the rock shadows
and rattlesnake paths,
feel the prayers.

Hidden somewhere in the line between
sky and horizon, something preaches:

You know, all things had to begin.
You know, all things began here.

Everything opens for our return.

For Merle Haggard on His 74th Birthday

i.

Fending against my first chickenhawk attack: men's room,
Oklahoma City bus station. He wore a yachting cap,
heavy glasses—teeth like bleached corn kernels. I ran to
the Trailways headed to Muskogee, safe in a tie-dyed
T-shirt, *Rolling Stone* tucked under my arm, safe, locked
in, safe, rolling down I-40, city receding, safe, fourteen-
years-old, trying to break with everything I knew.

ii.

I made that trip dozens of times. We were supposed to hate you
then. I never could. In my fantasies you were a highway
dad and poet. I wanted to be a poet more than anything.
We passed the gas station in Checotah, turning on to U.S
69. I knew those roads better than anything. I knew your
family came from Checotah, not Muskogee. Checotah
made even an Oildale boxcar look like relief.

iii.

My fat cousin and I swapped buses in Muskogee. I had smoked
marijuana by then. I also knew the inside of the Hilltop
Café, where you were considered a hero. My fat cousin
and I were the only white guys on the bus for Tahlequah.
The other riders were Indians and someone passed a bottle of
cheap wine. Soft white lines and I understood how someone
kept pushing highway songs. Safe.

iv.

You dug ditches and wired houses after Quentin. Then moved
on to poetry and diesel rhymes. Your face became a cliff
in the Sierras. I never liked manual labor either. And I've
done time in my own prisons. Computers, spreadsheets,
performance reviews—all my fluorescent-lit cellblocks.
The soft screws were brutal as any and never laid a single
hand on me.

v.

I took one big break in Taos before I hit thirty. Snow swirled the
plaza and in a sparse café, I heard "Ramblin' Fever" for
the first time. She sat bored. I leaped from the frozen
breakfast table and dived through the window. I ran
Through shard drifts, shoulder glances to see if the guards
chased me. At large, I swept down the Rio Grande
ahead of the spring melt, America embracing me.

But then I surrendered to myself, sentenced to solitary
confinement amidst comfortable houses, quiet cars, safe
streets, crossing guards, security patrols. Tonight I say
happy birthday, Hag, and wish I hadn't wasted so much
building a television life. I remember riding that bus out
of Muskogee all those years ago, passing the civic center,
your name out front—and feeling

Safe with Indians and wine. I've never really felt safe since,
always locked down.

Hospital Hill

Johnson grass and brick skirmish as the sun
Falls beyond hospital hill. I know this haze,
These insect songs, this red-tinged wind.

But I cannot accept this building collapse.
Nothing is right about it. I recall the lawn's
Manicure, not this greenbrier wasteland—

The window dazzle after autumn rain
Healing smells inside, nuns like black
Specters afloat on mirrored marble floors,

Starched nurses quick for their bidding. I recall
Benedictine Heights chiseled in majesty, not
This plywood, this rot, these Keep Out signs.

Once a neon cross tall as a school bus stood
Atop this place, shining a Gatsby green light
Toward all us east-siders, hope here in wounded

Wheat harvest country. No one knows what
Became of it, discarded with the nuns and nurses
Sometime during the for-profit age of Reagan.

Memory is my heroin. I ache to free the plywood
To find the place inside this dilapidation
Where my first breath died. I finger a brick,

But this time go no farther.
Highway thunder beckons
And I flee to the handlebars
To rumble back to Texas.

Driving to the Texas State Cemetery

You hear dead man's blues through building
Noise. Tired of being a slave, he wailed—
And you know that kind of surrender.
Submit now to the white Interstate heat: this is
The best the world can birth these days
If you choose to stay in the game—
That and hip-hop thuds, diseased trees,
Graceless graffiti, asphalt shivers,
Rotted porch planks, rusted chain link,
The sun nothing more than molded orange.
Beckon me this: a New Mexico pueblo
Where the phones sometimes don't work
And the Internet is a lunatic nightmare.
But we're far from that, here where adobe melts
In humidity foul as Houston and NAFTA
Trucks destroy the wind.

The old man captured
One thing near death two years ago:
Fallen flesh and crumbled bone mean
Nothing. Breathing persists after lungs fail.
We turn toward the new hole in the caliche,
Confront the swelter, push past the racket:

Abiding.

AFTERWORD

I loved that guy so much. What a shame. What a fucking shame . . .

—Chalo Gonzalez, Peckinpah's Friend

W.K. (Kip) Stratton is best known as the author of the nonfiction books *Backyard Brawl*, *Chasing the Rodeo*, *Boxing Shadows*, and the forthcoming *Floyd Patterson* (scheduled for publication in 2012 by Houghton Mifflin Harcourt), as well as for his magazine journalism for such publications as *GQ* and *Sports Illustrated*. But Stratton also has been writing poetry since he was a teenager, and as a college student, he took part in workshops and seminars led by N. Scott Momaday, James Dickey, Donald Hall, William Pitt Root, and William Stafford. Prior to this collection (his first), he has been somewhat reluctant to publish his verse, although some of these poems previously appeared (most in different form) in *Point Riders Great Plains Poetry Anthology*, *Territory of Oklahoma*, *Greenfield Review*, and *Cenizo Journal*. He lives in suburban Austin, Texas.

Photo by Brian H. Powell at R. Lord's Boxing Gym

CPSIA information can be obtained at www.ICGtesting.com
Printed in the USA
BVOW010747280911

272296BV00003B/137/P

9 780983 596875